D0630582

Jesus and I

Aloysius J. Heeg, S.J.

LOYOLA UNIVERSITY PRESS
Chicago 60657

Imprimatur: ✠ Albert Gregory Meyer
Archbishop of Chicago
November 20, 1958 (updated with permission)

Copyright 1942, © 1959, 1972
Loyola University Press
Printed in the United States of America
ISBN 0-8294-0214-4

TEACHER'S INTRODUCTION

Jesus and I incorporates not only the original narrative of *Jesus and I*, but also the question-and-answer text of the *First Communion Catechism* prepared from the *Baltimore Catechism.*

Jesus and I gives the teacher both a choice of method and a choice of material. If he wishes to present only what was in the original *Jesus and I*, he will teach the matter corresponding to the questions under the heading, "How many can you answer?" If he wants to teach only what was in the *First Communion Catechism*, he will confine himself to the matter corresponding to the questions "Can you also answer these?" See pages 132 to 138 for First Communion questions and answers.

Jesus and I is sufficiently flexible to meet the needs not only of children who normally receive their First Holy Communion at seven, but serves as well for those who are older.

Only the easier questions need be presented to the tiny tots. These questions can be readily recognized, for they are at the end of each lesson under the heading, "How many can you answer?"

This book has more than sufficient matter even for the exceptional class of older First Communicants. For their use the Confiteor and the Apostles' Creed are given. For them, too, are the simple summaries of the essentials of the commandments and the sacraments.

STUDENT'S NOTE

Here is a little book for you. If anyone asks you what it is all about, just say,

In this little book

1 I see and learn all about Jesus.
2 He teaches me my prayers.
3 He helps me with my catechism.
4 He prepares me for confession and
   Holy Communion.

PRAYERS

⟨ The Sign of the Cross

In the name of the Father, and of the Son, and of the Holy Spirit. Amen.

Prayer to My Guardian Angel

Angel of God, my Guardian dear,
To whom God's love entrusts me here,
Ever this day be at my side,
To light and guard, to rule and guide. Amen.

⟨ The Hail Mary

Hail Mary, full of grace, the Lord is with thee; blessed art thou among women, and blessed is the fruit of thy womb, Jesus.

Holy Mary, Mother of God, pray for us sinners, now and at the hour of our death. Amen.

⟨ The Lord's Prayer

Our Father who art in heaven, hallowed be thy name; thy kingdom come; thy will be done on earth as it is in heaven.

Give us this day our daily bread; and forgive us our trespasses as we forgive those who trespass

1

against us; and lead us not into temptation, but deliver us from evil. Amen.

The Confiteor

I confess to almighty God, and to you, my brothers and sisters, that I have sinned through my own fault: in my thoughts and in my words, in what I have done, and in what I have failed to do; and I ask Blessed Mary, ever virgin, all the angels and saints, and you, my brothers and sisters, to pray for me to the Lord our God.

May almighty God have mercy on us, forgive us our sins, and bring us to everlasting life. Amen.

The Apostles' Creed

I believe in God, the Father almighty, Creator of heaven and earth; and in Jesus Christ, his only Son, our Lord; who was conceived by the Holy Spirit; born of the Virgin Mary; suffered under Pontius Pilate, was crucified, died, and was buried. He descended into hell; the third day he arose again from the dead; he ascended into heaven, sits at the right hand of God, the Father almighty; from thence he shall come to judge the living and the dead.

I believe in the Holy Spirit; the Holy Catholic Church; the communion of saints; the forgiveness of sins; the resurrection of the body; and life everlasting. Amen.

A Brief Act of Contrition

O my God, I am sorry for all my sins, because they displease thee, who art all good and deserving of all my love. With thy help, I will sin no more. Amen.

A Longer Act of Contrition

O my God, I am heartily sorry for having offended thee, and I detest all my sins, because of thy just punishments, but most of all because they offend thee, my God, who art all-good and deserving of all my love. I firmly resolve, with the help of thy grace, to sin no more and to avoid the near occasions of sin. Amen.

Short Acts of Faith, Hope, and Love

O Jesus, I believe in you.
O Jesus, I hope in you.
O Jesus, I love you with all my heart.

An Act of Faith

O my God, I believe all the truths which the Holy Catholic Church teaches, because you have made them known.

An Act of Hope

O my God, because you are all-powerful, merciful, and faithful to your promises, I hope to be happy with you in heaven.

An Act of Love

O my God, because you are all-good, I love you with my whole heart and soul.

Morning Offering

O my God, I offer you every thought and word and act of today. Please bless the people of the whole world, especially my family and friends. And please, dear God, help me to be good today.

Daily Offering: Apostles of Prayer

Eternal and merciful Father, may my prayers, works, studies, joys, and sufferings help to restore all things in Christ. Alive with his spirit and yours

I offer them with the Eucharistic Sacrifice for the intentions of the Sacred Heart of Jesus and the Immaculate Heart of Mary, especially the sanctification and salvation of every person and the reunion of Christians. I include also the intentions of all Apostles of Prayer, our bishops, and our Holy Father, and in particular .... (the intention recommended for this month).

✗ The Glory Be to the Father

Glory be to the Father, and to the Son, and to the Holy Spirit. As it was in the beginning, is now, and ever shall be, world without end. Amen.

✗ The Blessing Before Meals

Bless us, O Lord, and these thy gifts which we are about to receive from thy bounty, through Christ our Lord. Amen.

Grace After Meals

We give thee thanks for all thy benefits, O almighty God, who livest and reignest forever. Amen.

May the souls of the faithful departed, through the mercy of God, rest in peace. Amen.

5

✗ The Seven Sacraments
and some things they do

1 BAPTISM

gives us a share in God's life; makes us children of God and members of his family; takes away original sin and personal sin.

2 CONFIRMATION

gives us the Holy Spirit in a special way; helps us to be strong Christians when we have to show others that we really believe in Christ and in his Church.

3 HOLY EUCHARIST

gives us Jesus in the Mass and Holy Communion; is a sign of our union with one another.

4 PENANCE

takes away our sins and helps us to live a good life.

5 ANOINTING OF THE SICK

helps us when we are very sick or in danger of death.

6

6 HOLY ORDERS

> makes men priests and helps them to take the place of Jesus in carrying on the life of the Church.

7 MATRIMONY

> blesses the marriage of two people and helps them to live the way they should.

The Ten Commandments
and some things they tell us to do

1 I AM THE LORD THY GOD; THOU SHALT NOT HAVE STRANGE GODS BEFORE ME.

> We should love God and pray to him.

2 THOU SHALT NOT TAKE THE NAME OF THE LORD THY GOD IN VAIN.

> We should love the name of God and use his name and the names of other holy persons, places, and things in the right way.

3 REMEMBER THAT THOU KEEP HOLY THE LORD'S DAY.

> We should go to Mass every Sunday and holy day or on the evening before.

4 HONOR THY FATHER AND THY MOTHER.

We should love and obey our parents and all who are over us.

5 THOU SHALT NOT KILL.

We should be kind and not quarrel and fight.

6 THOU SHALT NOT COMMIT ADULTERY.

We should be pure in all we see, hear, say, and do.

7 THOU SHALT NOT STEAL.

We should be honest and never damage or steal anything.

8 THOU SHALT NOT BEAR FALSE WITNESS AGAINST THY NEIGHBOR.

We should be truthful and never tell a lie.

9 THOU SHALT NOT COVET THY NEIGHBOR'S WIFE.

We should be pure in all we think and wish.

10 THOU SHALT NOT COVET THY NEIGHBOR'S GOODS.

We should be satisfied with what we have and not want what does not belong to us in a greedy or jealous way.

All for you

Who made all things? Who made the world and all the things in it? It was someone just as good as he can be. It was someone who loves me. It was someone who loves everyone in the whole world. It was God.

God is a spirit. He is just as beautiful and wonderful as he can be. God had no beginning; he always was. God will have no end; he will always be. God made all things out of nothing.

God is everywhere. I cannot see him because he is a spirit. God made all things. God sees all things. God knows all things. God can do all things.

God made me. God sees me. God knows me by name. He loves me. God is my Father.

God made me to show his goodness and to make me happy with him in heaven. To be happy with God in heaven I must know him, love him, and serve him in this world. I must also help others to know, love, and serve him.

God does everything for me. What can I do for him? I can pray; I can work; I can play. I can do everything for him.

So before everything I do, I will say with all my heart, "All for you."

HOW MANY CAN YOU ANSWER?

1 Who made all things?
2 Did God have a beginning?
3 Will God have an end?
4 How did God make all things?
5 Why can you not see God?

6 What does God see?
7 What can God do?
8 Who is God?
9 What does God do for you?
10 What can you do for God?
11 What prayer can you say to tell God you are doing everything for him?

CAN YOU ALSO ANSWER THESE?

12 Who made you?
13 Did God make all things?
14 Why did God make you?
15 What must you do to be happy with God in heaven?
16 Where is God?
17 Does God know all things?
18 Can God do all things?
19 Did God have a beginning?
20 Will God always be?

*In the name of the Father, and of the Son,
and of the Holy Spirit. Amen*

There is only one God, but in God there are three
Persons—the Father, the Son, and the Holy Spirit.

We call the three Persons in one God the Blessed
Trinity. We know that there are three Persons in one
God because we have God's word for it.

I show that I believe that there are three Persons
in one God when I make the sign of the cross and

12

say, "In the name of the Father, and of the Son, and of the Holy Spirit."

Later on I shall learn that God the Son came down to earth. He became man and died for us on the cross. I show that I believe this when I make the sign of the cross carefully.

The Father, the Son, and the Holy Spirit are equal in all things. The Father does everything for me. The Son does everything for me. The Holy Spirit does everything for me. How good God is!

When I start to bless myself, I say, "In the name of." God sees the sign. He hears the words. He knows that this is another way of telling him, "I am going to do this for you."

And that is the way I begin to pray.

HOW MANY CAN YOU ANSWER?

21 What are the names of the three Persons in God?
22 How do you show that you believe that there are three Persons in one God?
23 How do you show that you believe that God the Son became man and died for us on the cross?
24 Are the three Persons equal in all things?
25 What do the three Persons do for you?

26 What do you say when you start to bless yourself?
27 Who sees the sign of the cross you make?
28 Who hears the words you say?
29 What are you really telling God when you make the sign of the cross?
30 When do you make the sign of the cross?

CAN YOU ALSO ANSWER THESE?

31 Is there only one God?
32 How many Persons are there in God?
33 What do we call the three Persons in one God?
34 How do we know that there are three Persons in one God?

REVIEW QUESTIONS

Who made you?
Did God make all things?
Why did God make you?
What must you do to be happy with God in heaven?

Angel of God, my Guardian dear, to whom
God's love entrusts me here

God made the angels. God made all of them good. He made a most beautiful home for them. It is called heaven. God wanted all of the angels to be in heaven.

Some of the angels did not want to do what God told them. Since sin is disobedience to God's laws, the bad angels committed the first sin. That serious sin displeased God. He could not let the bad angels into heaven. He had to make a place where they could be punished and kept forever. That place is called hell. The bad angels had to be thrown into hell. The bad angels try to make me sin. "To sin" means to disobey God, to say no to what he asks me to do.

The good angels did what God wanted. That pleased God. He took them into heaven. The good angels want to keep me good. God gave me a good angel to take care of me. He is called my Guardian Angel. I cannot see my Guardian Angel because angels are spirits. I should love and pray to my Guardian Angel.

"To whom God's love entrusts me here" means that God loves me and tells the angel to take care of me here.

HOW MANY CAN YOU ANSWER?

35 Who made the angels?
36 Did he make all of the angels good?
37 What did God make for the angels?

38 Where did God want all of the angels to be?

39 Why were some of the angels not able to be in heaven?

40 What did God have to make for the bad angels?

41 What do the bad angels try to do?

42 What does "to sin" mean?

43 Why did God give you a good angel?

44 What is the good angel who takes care of you called?

45 Why can't you see your Guardian Angel?

46 How can you show your angel that you are grateful for his care?

47 What prayer do you know to your Guardian Angel?

48 What do these words mean: "To whom God's love entrusts me here"?

CAN YOU ALSO ANSWER THESE?

49 What is sin?

50 Who committed the first sin?

REVIEW QUESTIONS

Where is God?
Does God know all things?
Can God do all things?
Did God have a beginning?
Will God always be?

17

Is there only one God?

How many Persons are there in God?

What do we call the three Persons in one God?

How do we know that there are three Persons in
one God?

*Ever this day be at my side, to light and
guard, to rule and guide*

God made Adam and Eve. Adam was the first
man. Eve was the first woman. They were our first
parents. Like us they had a body and a soul.

God loved Adam and Eve and gave them many
gifts. The most wonderful gift that God gave them
was the gift of his own life in their souls. This is

called sanctifying grace. Sanctifying grace makes the soul holy and pleasing to God. It is a gift that makes the soul very bright and beautiful. It is a gift that makes the soul like God himself. Because God gave this gift to Adam and Eve, they became children in his family and could go to heaven.

At first Adam and Eve lived in a beautiful garden and were very happy. God wanted to let Adam and Eve show that they loved him and would obey him. God gave a special command to our first parents to test their love for him.

Then Lucifer, the leader of the bad angels, tricked Eve. He got Eve to tell him God's special command. The devil showed Eve how good it would be to do what God had told them not to do. Eve did what the devil wanted and so did Adam.

That was a serious sin. It spoiled everything. It took away from Adam and Eve that great gift of God's life in their souls. They were no longer holy and pleasing to God. Adam and Eve were driven out of that beautiful garden and had to die.

Our first parents, Adam and Eve, committed the first sin on earth. This sin is passed on to us from

Adam. This sin in us is called original sin. No one can go to heaven as long as he has this sin on his soul. To get to heaven we must have that great gift of God's life, sanctifying grace.

It was all their own fault. Yet God felt sorry for Adam and Eve and for us. He promised to send a Savior to make up for our sins and to get back for us that gift of sanctifying grace.

How we wish that Adam and Eve had listened to their Guardian Angels and not to the devil!

I ask my Guardian Angel to help me when I say, "Ever this day be at my side, to light and guard, to rule and guide."

HOW MANY CAN YOU ANSWER?

51 Who made Adam and Eve?
52 Who were Adam and Eve?
53 What was the most wonderful gift that God gave to Adam and Eve?
54 Did God give Adam and Eve a special command?
55 How did Lucifer trick Eve?
56 Did Eve listen to God or to the devil?
57 What happened to Adam and Eve because they disobeyed God?

58 Did our first parents commit the first sin on earth?
59 What is original sin?
60 Can anyone go to heaven as long as he has this sin on his soul?
61 What gift of God must we have to get to heaven?
62 Why did God promise to send a Savior?
63 What would the Savior do for us?
64 What do you wish Adam and Eve had done?
65 What do you ask your Guardian Angel to do when you say, "Ever this day be at my side, to light and guard, to rule and guide"?

CAN YOU ALSO ANSWER THESE?

66 Who committed the first sin on earth?
67 Is this sin passed on to us from Adam?
68 What is this sin in us called?

Hail Mary, full of grace, the Lord is with thee;
blessed art thou among women

Original sin is not the only kind of sin. No, there is another kind of sin, called actual sin. Actual sin is any sin which we ourselves commit.

After the sin of Adam and Eve it was very hard to be good. Many of the people disobeyed God's laws and had to be punished.

Some people tried to be good. They wanted to do everything that God asked. They prayed for the Savior to come.

After many years, the time came for God to send the Savior. The Savior was to be God the Son. He was to come into this world as a little baby. So God told the Angel Gabriel to go to Nazareth and ask Mary to be the Mother of the Savior.

Mary was the holiest woman that ever lived. She is called the Blessed Virgin Mary. The Blessed Virgin Mary was free from original sin. She was also free from every other sin. Her soul always had that great gift of sanctifying grace.

When the angel appeared to her, he said, "Hail, full of grace, the Lord is with thee; blessed art thou among women."

Grace makes the soul holy and pleasing to God. Mary's soul was so holy and pleasing to God that the angel called her "full of grace"!

Of all the women of the world, God picked out Mary to be his Mother. That is why the angel said, "The Lord is with thee; blessed art thou among women."

And so one of the Persons of the Blessed Trinity became man. Yes, the Second Person, the Son of God, became man. He became man to satisfy for the sins of all men and to help everybody to gain heaven. He came into this world to get back for us that great gift of sanctifying grace.

HOW MANY CAN YOU ANSWER?

69 Why did many of the people who lived after Adam and Eve sin?

70 What happened to the people who sinned?

71 Besides trying to be good, what did some of the people do?

72 Who was to be the Savior?

73 What did God tell the Angel Gabriel to do?

74 What did the angel say when he appeared to Mary?

75 Why did the angel call her "full of grace"?

76 Why did the angel say, "The Lord is with thee; blessed art thou among women"?

CAN YOU ALSO ANSWER THESE?

77 Did one of the Persons of the Blessed Trinity become man?

78 Why did God the Son become man?

79 Was anyone ever free from original sin?

80 Is original sin the only kind of sin?
81 What is actual sin?
82 What does grace do to the soul?

REVIEW QUESTIONS

Is there only one God?
How many Persons are there in God?
What do we call the three Persons in one God?
How do we know that there are three Persons in
    one God?

And blessed is the fruit of thy womb, Jesus

After the angel returned to heaven, Mary went to see her cousin Elizabeth. The Holy Spirit let Saint Elizabeth know that Mary was the Mother of the Savior. Saint Elizabeth was the first one to say to Mary, "Blessed is the fruit of thy womb."

After that Mary and Joseph had to go all the way to Bethlehem. When they got there, they could not find any place to stay. The people in the houses said, "There is no room." So Mary and Joseph had to go into a poor stable.

In that poor stable the Savior was born. Angels told some shepherds all about it, and they went over to see him.

The little baby they saw was the Son of God made man. The name of the Son of God made man is Jesus Christ. He was named Jesus because "Jesus" means Savior.

Jesus was born on the first Christmas Day, more than nineteen hundred years ago.

The Mother of Jesus is the Blessed Virgin Mary. In the Hail Mary we say to her, "Blessed is the fruit of thy womb, Jesus." These words mean blessed is your child, Jesus.

HOW MANY CAN YOU ANSWER?

83 Where did Mary go after the angel returned to heaven?

84 What did the Holy Spirit let Saint Elizabeth know?

85 Who was the first to say to Mary, "Blessed is the fruit of thy womb"?

86 After Mary came back from Elizabeth's house,
   where did she and Joseph have to go?
87 What happened when they got to Bethlehem?
88 Why did Mary and Joseph go into a poor stable?
89 Where was the Savior born?
90 What did the angels do?
91 Why was the Savior named Jesus?
92 What do these words mean: "Blessed is the fruit of
   thy womb, Jesus"?

CAN YOU ALSO ANSWER THESE?

93 What is the name of the Son of God made man?
94 When was Jesus born?
95 Who is the Mother of Jesus?

REVIEW QUESTIONS

Did one of the Persons of the Blessed Trinity
   become man?
Why did God the Son become man?
Was anyone ever free from original sin?
Is original sin the only kind of sin?
What is actual sin?
What does grace do to the soul?

Holy Mary, Mother of God

Far, far away three wise men saw a beautiful star. It seemed to say, "Come, follow me!" The wise men got ready and followed the star. It showed them the way to Bethlehem. It stopped right over the place where Jesus was.

The three wise men were very happy when they went in and saw Jesus. They knelt down before him and gave him beautiful gifts. Mary was glad when she knew that the wise men loved Jesus.

The three kings were also happy because they saw Mary. Mary always loved Jesus with all her heart. Mary was always very, very holy. She never had a sin on her soul. That is why we call her Holy Mary.

Jesus is both God and man. We call Mary "Mother of God" because Mary is the Mother of Jesus, and Jesus is God. Mary is also our mother. She loves us, and we love her.

Jesus did not have a real father on earth, but Saint Joseph took care of him just like a real father. We love Saint Joseph too. He was always so good to Jesus and Mary. We call Joseph the foster father of Jesus.

HOW MANY CAN YOU ANSWER?

96 What did the three wise men see?
97 What did they do?
98 How did the wise men feel when they saw Jesus?
99 Why was Mary glad to see the wise men?
100 Why do we call Mary "Holy Mary"?
101 Why do we call her "Mother of God"?

102 Why does Mary love us?
103 Who is Jesus' real father?
104 Who took care of Jesus just like a father?
105 Why do we love Saint Joseph?

CAN YOU ALSO ANSWER THIS?

106 Is Jesus Christ both God and man?

REVIEW QUESTIONS

When was Jesus born?
Who is the Mother of Jesus?

Pray for us sinners

There was also a wicked king. His name was Herod. He was not like the three wise men who loved Jesus so much. He wanted to kill Jesus.

During the night God sent an angel to tell Saint Joseph what Herod wanted to do. Joseph was asleep when the angel came. So the angel said, "Get up, take the Child and his Mother with you, and escape into Egypt." Saint Joseph got up right away. Before anyone knew it, he had Jesus and Mary far, far away.

Then King Herod sent his soldiers to Bethlehem. They killed all the baby boys. They thought they had killed Jesus too, but he was safe with Mary and Joseph.

How Mary must have prayed on their way to Egypt! She was so good, she would even pray for King Herod. Surely none of us will ever be as big a sinner as King Herod. But we are all called sinners because we sometimes do what is wrong.

Mary wants us always to be good. She will help us if we pray to her. She is glad to hear us say, "Pray for us sinners."

HOW MANY CAN YOU ANSWER?

107 Can you tell the story about the wicked king?
108 What was his name?
109 What did King Herod want to do?
110 How did God protect Jesus, Mary, and Joseph?
111 What did the angel tell Joseph to do?
112 How did Joseph act when he received the angel's message?

113 Why did King Herod send his soldiers
to Bethlehem?
114 What did the soldiers think they had done?
115 Why would Mary pray for King Herod?
116 Why are we called sinners?
117 How does Mary want us to act?
118 Who will help us if we pray to her?
119 What is she glad to hear us say?

REVIEW QUESTION

What is sin?

Now

Jesus, Mary, and Joseph stayed in Egypt until an angel came and told them that the wicked king was dead. Then they went back to their own little town of Nazareth.

Jesus, Mary, and Joseph were poor, and they had to work hard. But their home was very happy because they were so holy. They are called the Holy Family.

Jesus loved Mary and Joseph. He always did what they told him. He helped them all he could.

Jesus showed us how to be good. He prayed well; he worked well; he played well. Jesus wants us to do as he did. He wants us to pray well, to work well, to play well.

Mary and Joseph did everything well because they did everything for Jesus. We can do everything well if we do everything for Jesus. When we want to do something for Jesus, we can say, "All for you, O Jesus."

Mary loves to see us do everything for Jesus. She hurries to help us when we pray the Hail Mary and really mean that little word "now."

HOW MANY CAN YOU ANSWER?

120 How long did Jesus, Mary, and Joseph stay in Egypt?
121 Where did Jesus, Mary, and Joseph go after they left Egypt?
122 Why did Jesus, Mary, and Joseph have to work hard?
123 Why was their home happy?
124 What are they called?

125 How did Jesus show that he loved Mary
and Joseph?
126 Did Jesus show us how to be good?
127 Can you tell three things that Jesus did well?
128 What can we do to be like Jesus?
129 Why did Mary and Joseph do everything well?
130 How can we do everything well?
131 What can we say when we want to do something
for Jesus?
132 What does Mary do when we pray the Hail Mary
and really mean that little word "now"?

And at the hour of our death. Amen

Jesus, Mary, and Joseph loved to pray. They often spoke to God their loving Father. At times they praised God and told him how great and wonderful he is. At other times they asked God for whatever they needed. Jesus, Mary, and Joseph always remembered to thank God for his goodness to them. And sometimes they even prayed prayers telling their heavenly Father how sorry they were for evil and sin in the world.

When Jesus was twelve years old, they walked many, many miles just to pray in the Temple at Jerusalem. Then Jesus was lost. Mary and Joseph prayed and searched until they found him. They found him in the Temple, listening to the great teachers and asking them questions. Those teachers would have liked to keep Jesus with them all the time. But when Mary and Joseph asked Jesus to go back home, he went with them right away.

Jesus never got tired of helping Mary and Joseph. He stayed with them at home until he was about thirty years old.

Saint Joseph died a happy death because Jesus and Mary were with him. Jesus and Mary will also be with us when we die if we often say with all our heart those words of the Hail Mary, "Pray for us sinners, now and at the hour of our death. Amen."

133 Who loved to pray?

134 Name four kinds of prayer Jesus, Mary, and Joseph used.

135 What did the Holy Family do when Jesus was twelve years old?

136 What happened to Jesus in Jerusalem?

137 What did Mary and Joseph do when Jesus was lost?

138 Where did they find Jesus?

139 What would those teachers have liked to do?

140 What did Jesus do when Mary and Joseph asked him to go back home?

141 How long did Jesus stay at home?

142 Why did Saint Joseph die a happy death?

143 What should we often pray if we want Jesus and Mary to be with us when we die?

REVIEW QUESTIONS

Does God know all things?

Is Jesus Christ both God and man?

41

Our Father who art in heaven

When Jesus was about thirty years old, he began to teach the people. Then he picked out twelve men. He wanted them to be with him all the time. He was going to make them his first priests. They are called his apostles.

One day the apostles saw Jesus praying. He prayed so well that they wanted to learn to pray just as he did. So one of them went up to Jesus and said, "Lord, teach us to pray."

Jesus was glad. He told them to pray like this, "Our Father who art in heaven . . ." And so he went on until he finished the prayer. We now call the prayer Jesus taught us the Our Father.

"Our Father," it begins. Jesus wants us to remember that the good God is really the Father of us all. He loves us as his own children!

"Who art in heaven" are the next words. They tell us that God lives in heaven. Although God is everywhere, we can see him only in heaven. Heaven is God's home. It will be our home too, if we live good Christian lives here on earth.

HOW MANY CAN YOU ANSWER?

144 What did Jesus do when he was about thirty years old?

145 Why did he pick out twelve men?

146 What was he going to make them?

147 What are they called?

148 How did Jesus pray?

149 What did one of the apostles ask Jesus to do?

150 How did Jesus tell them to pray?

151 What do we now call the prayer that Jesus taught us to pray?
152 What does Jesus want us to remember when we say, "Our Father"?
153 How does God love us?
154 What do the words "who art in heaven" tell us?
155 What is heaven?

REVIEW QUESTION

Why did God make you?

44

Hallowed be thy name; thy kingdom come

Jesus told a story about two men who went to the Temple to pray. One was called a Pharisee. The other was called a Publican.

The Pharisee was very proud. He was a sinful man, but he wanted everyone to think that he was very good. When he prayed, he only wanted to show off before all the people. He did not honor

God when he prayed. He just praised himself. He said, "I thank you God that I am not grasping and unjust like the rest of mankind . . ."

The Publican was not proud at all. When he went to the Temple, he wanted to please God. He did not care what people thought. He bowed his head and struck his breast and said, "O God, be merciful to me the sinner."

Jesus wants us to pray like the Publican and not like the Pharisee. When we pray, we talk to God. When we talk to God, we should think of what we are saying.

When we say, "Hallowed be thy name," we wish that God may be honored and loved by all. When we say, "Thy kingdom come," we pray that God may be our king both here and in heaven.

HOW MANY CAN YOU ANSWER?

156 Why did Jesus tell a story about two men who went to the Temple to pray?
157 What were the two men called?
158 What kind of man was the Pharisee?
159 How did the Pharisee pray?
160 How was the Publican different from the Pharisee?

161 How did the Publican pray?

162 How does Jesus want us to pray?

163 What is prayer?

164 What should we do when we talk to God?

165 What do we wish when we say, "Hallowed be thy name"?

166 What do we pray for when we say, "Thy kingdom come"?

Thy will be done on earth as it is in heaven

One day Jesus told the apostles to cross a lake. He
was very tired, and he went to sleep in the back of
the boat. While he slept, a big storm came up. The
waves rushed into the little boat, and it began to
sink. The apostles became afraid. They turned to
Jesus. They woke him up and said, "Save us!" Then
Jesus stood up. He stretched out his arms and said,
"Peace, be still!" And right away the storm was still.

Jesus is God! The storm did the will of God when it obeyed Jesus. The apostles did the will of God when they tried to cross the lake. We do the will of God when we do what God wants. If we find it hard to do what God wants, we can ask Jesus to help us. Jesus himself had to do many things that were hard. When they were very, very hard, he said, "Thy will be done."

The angels and saints in heaven always do what God wants, and that is what we should do on earth. That is why we say, "Thy will be done on earth as it is in heaven."

HOW MANY CAN YOU ANSWER?

167 Can you tell the story about Jesus and the storm?
168 What happened when Jesus slept?
169 What did the apostles do?
170 What did they say to Jesus?
171 What did Jesus do?
172 What happened to the storm?
173 Who is Jesus?
174 How did the storm do the will of God?
175 How did the apostles do the will of God?
176 When do we do the will of God?

177 What can we do if we find it hard to do what
God wants?

178 What did Jesus say when things were very,
very hard?

179 Why do we say, "Thy will be done on earth as it is
in heaven"?

Give us this day our daily bread

The people loved to listen to Jesus. They sometimes stayed with him all day long. One day they were in a place where there was nothing to eat. The only one who had brought much food along was a little boy.

One of the apostles saw this little boy. He said to Jesus, "There is a young boy here that has five bar-

51

ley loaves and two fishes, but what are these among so many?" "Bring them here to me," said Jesus.

Then all the people sat down and watched Jesus. Jesus gave thanks. He looked up to heaven. He blessed those five loaves and two fishes, and made them enough so the apostles could feed more than five thousand people.

The next day Jesus promised to give his own flesh and blood to feed the whole world. Jesus can do this because he is God.

When we say, "Give us this day our daily bread," God is willing to give us everything we need for our soul and body. He always gives us more than we ask for.

HOW MANY CAN YOU ANSWER?

180 Why were so many people with Jesus?
181 Can you tell the story about the people having nothing to eat?
182 What did an apostle say to Jesus?
183 What did Jesus say to him?
184 What did the people do?
185 What did Jesus do to the loaves and fishes?
186 What did Jesus promise the next day?

187 Why can Jesus do this?

188 What is God willing to give us when we say, "Give us this day our daily bread"?

REVIEW QUESTIONS

Can God do all things?

Is Jesus Christ both God and man?

And forgive us our trespasses
as we forgive those who trespass against us

Jesus told a story about a king who was going to punish a servant. The servant fell down on his knees and begged the king to forgive him. The king felt sorry for the servant and forgave him.

Afterwards that servant would not forgive someone else. The king found this out. It made him very angry. He had the servant punished and would not forgive him any more.

In the same way, God will punish us if we do not forgive others.

When we say, "Forgive us our trespasses," we ask God to forgive us for having offended him.

When we say, "As we forgive those who trespass against us," we ask God to forgive us in the same way that we forgive those who hurt us.

Our sins are trespasses against God. They offend him very much. We should often ask God to forgive them. We do this if we often say the Our Father and mean what we say.

HOW MANY CAN YOU ANSWER?

189 What did a king want to do to one of his servants?
190 What did the servant ask from the king?
191 Why did the king forgive the servant?
192 Why did the king change his mind about forgiving the servant?
193 What will happen to us if we do not forgive others?
194 What do we ask God to do when we say, "Forgive us our trespasses"?

195 What do we tell God when we say, "As we forgive those who trespass against us"?

196 What is another word for sins?

REVIEW QUESTIONS

What is sin?
Who committed the first sin?
Who committed the first sin on earth?

And lead us not into temptation,
but deliver us from evil. Amen

Before Jesus began to teach, he stayed in a desert for forty days and forty nights. During all that time he fasted and prayed.

Then the devil came and tempted him. Jesus would not do anything the devil wanted. So he could not make Jesus sin. Jesus even drove him away. After that angels came to help Jesus.

The devil tempts us when he tries to get us to do what is wrong. It is not a sin to be tempted. As long as we do not do what the devil wants, everything is all right.

If we pray, God will help us.

When we say, "Lead us not into temptation," we pray that God will not let us sin.

When we say, "Deliver us from evil," we ask God to keep us from harm.

"Amen," we say at the end of the Our Father. The Our Father is our Lord's own prayer.

HOW MANY CAN YOU ANSWER?

197 Why did Jesus stay in the desert?
198 What word means that Jesus did not eat?
199 What happened after the forty days of fasting?
200 Why could not the devil make Jesus sin?
201 When does the devil tempt us?
202 Is it a sin to be tempted?
203 Who will help us when we are tempted?
204 What do we pray for when we say, "Lead us not into temptation"?

205 What do we ask God to do when we say, "Deliver us from evil"?

206 What is our Lord's own prayer?

REVIEW QUESTIONS

Is original sin the only kind of sin?

What is actual sin?

*O my God, I am heartily sorry for having offended thee,
and I detest all my sins*

A woman named Mary Magdalene was very sorry
for her sins. She knew that her sins offended Jesus,
and she wanted to make up for them. So she found
the house where Jesus was taking dinner. She did
not care what the other people would think. She just
wanted to see Jesus and tell him how sorry she was.
She went right in. She knelt down before Jesus.

She cried so hard that her tears washed his holy feet. To dry them she used her beautiful hair. Jesus was pleased. He turned to her and said, "Your sins are forgiven."

Mary Magdalene did not have to cry to be sorry, but she was so sorry that she could not help crying. When Mary heard Jesus' words, "Your sins are forgiven," her heart was filled with joy and peace. She knew that she was united more closely than before with God who loved her.

I am heartily sorry for my sins if I can truly say, "I wish I had not sinned. I would like to take my sins back. I do not want to sin again."

"To be heartily sorry" means to be really sorry. "To offend" God means to displease God. "To detest" sin means to hate sin. I should hate my sins. Each time I sin, I say no to God. I do not do what he wants me to do.

There are two kinds of actual sin: mortal sin and venial sin. Mortal sin is a deadly sin. Blasphemy, murder, adultery, and other big sins are mortal. Mortal sin causes us to lose God's life in our souls. It makes us enemies of God.

Venial sin is a lesser sin. Venial sin does not make us enemies of God or rob our souls of his life, but venial sin does displease God. Examples of venial sins are lying, being mean to others, disobeying my parents or others who take care of me.

Every sin should make me heartily sorry, because every sin displeases God who is so good and loving to his children.

HOW MANY CAN YOU ANSWER?

207 How did Mary Magdalene feel about her sins?
208 Why was she sorry for her sins?
209 What did Mary Magdalene do to let Jesus know that she was sorry?
210 Did she have to cry to be sorry?
211 What words of Jesus filled Mary Magdalene's heart with joy and peace?
212 When are you heartily sorry for your sins?
213 What does "to offend" mean?
214 What does "to detest" mean?
215 Why should I be sorry for every sin?

CAN YOU ALSO ANSWER THESE?

216 How many kinds of actual sin are there?
217 What is mortal sin?

218 What is venial sin?

219 Does venial sin make us enemies of God or rob our souls of his life?

220 Does venial sin displease God?

REVIEW QUESTION

Is Jesus Christ both God and man?

Because of thy just punishments

Jesus told a story about a rich man and a beggar.
The rich man was very bad. He would not help the
poor beggar. When the rich man died he did not
have God's life in his soul. He did not belong to the
family of God. So he could not enter heaven. The
evil rich man suffered for his sins and selfishness in
hell. No one could help the rich man any more.

64

Little children usually displease God in little ways. Grown-up people sometimes offend God in a big way. If someone does offend God in a big way, he should be afraid. Why? Because until he tells God he is really sorry for the mortal sin, he is God's enemy. If he dies before he is sorry, he will never see God, his Father. He will never see Mary, his mother. He will never see the angels. He will have to suffer in hell forever and ever.

If a person goes to hell, it will be his own fault. Jesus came on earth just to help everyone to go to heaven. Jesus does not wish to have anyone even go to purgatory. Purgatory is a place where sins have to be made up for before a person can go to heaven. The souls in purgatory suffer but they are also happy. They know that they will see God after their punishment for sinning is over.

"Because of thy just punishments" means because I do not want to make you punish me either in this world or in the next.

Mortal sin is a deadly sin. Mortal sin makes us enemies of God and robs us of his life. Like the rich man, those who die in mortal sin are punished forever. They must suffer in hell. To reach heaven and belong to God's family we must have the great gift of God's life, sanctifying grace.

HOW MANY CAN YOU ANSWER?

221 Can you tell the story that Jesus told about a rich man and a beggar?
222 What happened to the rich man when he died?
223 Why should people who commit big sins be afraid?
224 Whose fault will it be if we go to hell?
225 Why did Jesus come to earth?
226 What is purgatory?
227 What do these words mean: "Because of thy just punishments"?

CAN YOU ALSO ANSWER THESE?

228 What does mortal sin do to us?
229 What happens to those who die in mortal sin?

REVIEW QUESTIONS

Why did God the Son become man?
How many kinds of actual sin are there?
What is mortal sin? venial sin?
Does venial sin make us enemies of God or rob our souls of his life?
Does venial sin displease God?

*But most of all because they offend thee,
my God, who art all-good*

For three years Jesus taught the people how to love our heavenly Father and to love others too. But some men who did not believe in Jesus' message wanted to have him out of the way. Jesus knew they planned to put him to death. But he also knew that

67

by dying he could make up for the sins of men and help all people belong to God's family once again.

Jesus never gets tired of showing his love for us, even though it is our own sins that offend him so much. That is why we say we are sorry for our sins, "Most of all because they offend thee, my God, who art all-good."

The night before he died, Jesus gathered his apostles together at a special meal. It was at this Last Supper that Jesus made the apostles the first priests. After Jesus died the priests would take his place and carry on the life of the Church. During this first Mass, Jesus changed bread and wine into his own body and blood. He gave priests the power to do this also.

This gift to us is called the sacrament of the Holy Eucharist or the Blessed Sacrament. A sacrament is an outward sign, instituted by Christ to give grace. This is one of the seven special helps Jesus has given us to be strong Catholics. Through the sacraments we receive God's life into our souls.

The Holy Eucharist is the sacrament of the body and blood of our Lord Jesus Christ. It is Holy Communion. Jesus becomes present in the Holy Eucharist during the sacrifice of the Mass. When we assist at Mass, Jesus lets us offer up with him his death upon the cross. We give gifts to God, and God gives gifts to us. The best gift we give God is Jesus dying for us on the cross. And the best gift God gives to us is Jesus in Holy Communion This is the sacrament of God's love for us.

HOW MANY CAN YOU ANSWER?

230 What did Jesus do for three years?
231 Why did some men want to kill Jesus?
232 What did Jesus know he would do by his death?
233 Why do we say we are sorry for our sins, "Most of all because they offend thee, my God, who art all-good"?
234 What did Jesus do the evening before he died?
235 Who said the first Mass?
236 What did Jesus do with some bread and wine?
237 Who were the first priests?
238 After Jesus died, who would take his place and carry on the work of the Church?
239 What power did Jesus give priests?

240 What do we offer to God when we assist at holy Mass?

241 What gift does God give us during Mass?

CAN YOU ALSO ANSWER THESE?

242 What is a sacrament?

243 What is the sacrament of the Holy Eucharist?

244 When does Jesus Christ become present in the Holy Eucharist?

NOTE. If you want to know what the seven sacraments are and some things they do, please turn to pages 6 to 7. You will learn more about questions 243 and 244 when you study what is on pages 117 to 123 and 128 to 131.

And deserving of all my love

After the Last Supper Jesus went into a garden to pray. He knew that we should be punished for our sins. But he took our place to be punished for us. While he prayed, he saw all our sins. He saw all that he would suffer before he died. He knew how ungrateful we would be even after he had suffered for us. All of this made Jesus feel so afraid that while he prayed a sweat of blood came over him.

71

Then some of the enemies of Jesus came and took him away.

The next day was the first Good Friday. Jesus was tied up and whipped. A crown of thorns was pressed around his head. Then Jesus was made to carry a heavy wooden cross up Mount Calvary. Finally, he was fastened to the cross with nails. For three long hours Jesus suffered for us on that cross. During that time Jesus prayed for those who hated him and he even forgave his enemies. Jesus suffered and then died for our sins. How terrible is sin! How great and good is Jesus!

Dear Jesus, I am sorry that I have ever sinned. You are so good "and deserving of all my love."

"Deserving of all my love" means Jesus should have all my love.

Jesus is God the Son. He became man to satisfy for the sins of men and to help everybody to gain heaven. Jesus satisfied for the sins of all men by his sufferings and death on the cross.

By dying for us on the cross, Jesus won for us the great gift of sanctifying grace, God's own life. He helped us become children in God's family again.

245 Where did Jesus go after the Last Supper?
246 In whose place was Jesus going to die?
247 What did Jesus see while he prayed?
248 What came over Jesus' body because he felt
 so afraid?
249 What did the enemies of Jesus do to him?
250 What was pressed around his head?
251 Where did Jesus carry the cross?
252 What happened when they got to the top
 of the hill?
253 How did Jesus show that he loved even
 his enemies?
254 What does "deserving of all my love" mean?
255 What great gift did Jesus win back for us by his
 death on the cross?

CAN YOU ALSO ANSWER THIS?

256 How did Jesus satisfy for the sins of all men?

REVIEW QUESTIONS

Did one of the Persons of the Blessed Trinity
 become man?
What is the name of the Son of God
 made man?
Is Jesus Christ both God and man?

Why did God the Son become man?
What is sin?

NOTE. The next two lessons will tell you a little about the sacrament of penance. If you want to learn much more, please study pages 98 to 116 and 124 to 127. On page 98 there is a prayer that has in it the answer to question 290. On page 127 there is something to help you remember the answer to question 291.

I firmly resolve, with the help of thy grace, to sin no more

Three days after Jesus was buried, he came to life again. We call this the resurrection. The day Jesus rose from the dead was the first Easter.

Some holy women went out to his grave, but when they got there, an angel said, "He is not here." He was away, making his Mother and all his friends happy.

75

But how was Jesus going to make us happy? He knew we really cannot be happy and at peace if we have sins on our souls. That evening he went to the apostles and gave them the sacrament of forgiveness. Jesus said, "Whose sins you shall forgive they are forgiven them." That is how Jesus gave priests the power to take away our sins and make us at peace with God, others, and ourselves.

Sin is the worst thing in the world. But even if a sin is serious, the priest can take it away because of the power Jesus gave him. But we must be truly sorry for this sin and tell it in confession.

"I firmly resolve" means I really promise. When we want to do what is right God helps us. That is why we say, "With the help of thy grace." Grace is the name of the help that God gives. "To sin no more" means not to sin again.

When we go to confession we receive the sacrament of penance. This is also called the sacrament of forgiveness. In the sacrament of penance the sins committed after baptism are forgiven.

I have received the sacrament of baptism. Baptism washed away original sin from my soul and made it rich in the grace of God. Baptism gave me that great gift of God's life that was lost for us by Adam. It made me a child of God and a member of his family.

After baptism that great gift of God's life can be lost again. It is lost by committing mortal sin. But how good God is! He will give that great gift back even when it has been lost again. He does this through the sacrament of penance.

Most little boys and girls have not lost that great gift of sanctifying grace by mortal sin. When they go to confession they have only venial sins to confess. Then God gives them more and more of his grace, and they become even more holy and pleasing to him.

HOW MANY CAN YOU ANSWER?

257 What happened three days after Jesus was buried?
258 On what day do we remember Jesus' resurrection from the dead?
259 Who went out to Jesus' grave early in the morning?
260 What happened when they got there?
261 Where was Jesus?
262 When are we not able to be really happy?

263 What was Jesus' Easter gift to us?

264 Who received the power to forgive sin?

265 What must we do to have mortal sins forgiven?

266 Why do we confess our venial sins?

267 What does "I firmly resolve" mean?

268 Why do we say, "With the help of thy grace"?

269 What is grace?

270 What does "to sin no more" mean?

CAN YOU ALSO ANSWER THESE?

271 What sacrament have you received?

272 What did baptism do for you?

273 What is the sacrament of penance?

And to avoid the near occasions of sin

Jesus told a story about a boy who left his father's home. His father was very sad to see the boy go, but the boy insisted upon having his share of the family money to spend as he wanted.

Before long he had many friends who helped him spend his money foolishly. They got into all kinds of trouble. Once the boy's money was spent, his friends

79

left him alone, with nothing at all. He had no home, no money, and nothing to eat. The boy was finally able to get work feeding pigs.

For a long time he thought about how foolish he had been; how wrong to do the things he had done. The boy thought about returning to his father and asking to be a servant on his father's farm. Even the servants were treated better than he was being treated. He would not even ask to be treated as a son. He was so sorry for what he had done to his good father and how bad he had acted. The boy returned to his father's farm.

Each day the man had walked to the end of the yard to look and see if his son was coming home. Each day he returned to the house, very sad. How he missed his son! Then one day his son came home. How very happy the father was!

The father and his boy hugged and kissed each other and cried because they were so happy to be back together. The boy told his father how bad he had been, but the good father forgave his son everything.

Jesus wants us to remember that when we sin, we go away from him. But if we are sorry for our sins and do not want them any more, we can come back to him. Jesus wants us to come back to him more than the father wanted his son to return. Jesus wants us to meet him in the sacrament of forgiveness.

The priest takes the place of Jesus when we go to confession. We say to him, "Bless me, Father. I have sinned. My last confession was ...." And then we tell him our sins. We can also tell how many times we committed each sin, but this will be necessary only when the sin is mortal.

After we have confessed our sins, the priest will give us a penance to do. The penance might be to say some special prayers, or it might be to do some action. After confession we should be glad to say or do our penance because it helps to make up for our sins.

After confession I try to avoid the near occasions of sin. "To avoid" means to keep away from. "Near occasions of sin" are any persons, places, or things that easily get me to sin.

To receive the sacrament of penance I must:
1 Find out my sins.
2 Be sorry for my sins.
3 Make up my mind not to sin again.
4 Tell my sins to the priest.
5 Do the penance the priest gives me.

I make my confession in this way:
1 I go into the confessional and kneel.
2 I make the sign of the cross and say, "Bless me, Father. I have sinned."
3 I say, "This is my first confession" (or, "It has been a week, or a month, or ...., since my last confession").
4 I confess my sins.
5 I listen to what the priest tells me.
6 I say the act of contrition or listen to the words of absolution. This depends on the priest and on what he wants me to do.

After leaving the confessional, I thank God for forgiving my sins. I say the prayers which the priest gave me as a penance. If my penance is to do some act, I ask God to help me remember to do it as soon as I have a chance.

274 Can you tell the story that Jesus told about a boy who left his father's home?

275 What did the boy take with him when he left home?

276 Why were the boy's friends not really good friends?

277 What did the boy think about while he was feeding the pigs?

278 How did he feel about what he had done?

279 What did the boy make up his mind to do?

280 What did the father do to the boy when he came home?

281 What do we do when we sin?

282 In what sacrament does Jesus forgive our sins the way the father forgave his son?

283 Whose place does the priest take?

284 What do we say to the priest when we begin?

285 And then what do we tell him?

286 What do we call the prayers or the action that the priest will tell us to do?

287 After confession what should we be glad to do?

288 What does "to avoid" mean?

289 What are near occasions of sin?

290 What must you do to receive the sacrament of penance?

291 How do you make your confession?

292 What do you do after leaving the confessional?

O Jesus, I believe in you

Jesus always wanted to help all the people who would live after him. So it was now time to start his Church. Long before, he had picked out one of his apostles and named him Peter. "Peter" means a rock. And Jesus had said to him, "Thou art Peter; and upon this rock I will build my Church."

85

Jesus now kept his promise. He started the Catholic Church and made Saint Peter the first pope. The pope is the head of the Church. He takes the place of Jesus on earth. When we do what the pope and the Catholic Church tell us, we do what Jesus himself wants us to do.

Jesus wants us all to be good Catholics. We became Catholics when we were baptized. Baptism took the sin of Adam from our souls and made us children of God.

The Church tells us that we must go to Mass every Sunday or the evening before. It is at this time that we worship God our Father and join with other members of his family in praising him. A good Catholic is glad to do this for Jesus.

We believe what Jesus and his Church tell us, for it must be true. "O Jesus, I believe in you."

Jesus helps all men to gain heaven through the Catholic Church. The Catholic Church helps us to gain heaven especially through the sacraments. I have received the sacrament of baptism. I am preparing to receive the sacraments of penance, Holy Eucharist, and confirmation.

293 What did Jesus do because he wanted to help all the people who would live after him?

294 Whom did Jesus choose to be the leader of his Church?

295 What does the name "Peter" mean?

296 What had Jesus said to him?

297 What did Jesus make Peter?

298 Who is the pope?

299 Whose place does the pope take?

300 What happens when we do what the pope tells us?

301 What does Jesus want us to be?

302 When did we become Catholics?

303 What did baptism do?

304 Who tells us that we must go to Mass every Sunday or on Saturday evening?

305 Why is a good Catholic glad to go to Mass on Sundays?

306 Why do we believe what Jesus tells us?

307 How can you tell Jesus you believe in him?

CAN YOU ALSO ANSWER THESE?

308 How does Jesus help all men to gain heaven?

309 How does the Catholic Church help us to gain heaven?

310 Are you preparing to receive other sacraments?

Why did God the Son become man?
What is a sacrament?
What sacrament have you received?
What is the sacrament of penance?

NOTE. In the Apostles' Creed you can find the chief truths taught by Jesus Christ through the Catholic Church. Please see pages 2 to 3.

O Jesus, I hope in you

After Jesus gave us the Catholic Church to take care of us, he went back to his Father in heaven.

In heaven his Father has everything we like. Everybody is just as happy as he can be. No one is poor; no one is sick; no one is ever sad.

Heaven is that most beautiful home where Jesus himself now lives. And just think of it! Jesus loves us so much that he wants us to live there too. He

89

wishes to have us for his brothers and sisters. And for how long? Forever and forever!

At the end of the world our bodies will come back to life again. And if our souls are in heaven, our bodies will go there too.

But Jesus cannot take us into heaven unless we are good. We can all be good because Jesus promised to help us. That is why we say, "O Jesus, I hope in you."

Jesus will take us into heaven if we have God's life in our souls when we die. The more grace we have in our souls when we die, the happier we will be in heaven.

Ten days after Jesus returned to heaven, he sent the Holy Spirit to the apostles. The Holy Spirit made the apostles strong. I will receive the Holy Spirit in a special way in the sacrament of confirmation.

Confirmation, through the coming of the Holy Spirit, will make me a witness of Jesus Christ. It will help me to be as strong as a soldier when I have to show by my life that I really believe in Jesus and in his Church.

311 Where did Jesus go after he gave us the Catholic Church to take care of us?

312 Why is everyone happy in heaven?

313 What is heaven?

314 For how long does Jesus want us to live in heaven as his brothers and sisters?

315 What will happen to our bodies at the end of the world?

316 If we want to go to heaven, how should we live?

317 Why can we be good even if at times it is hard?

318 Why do we pray, "O Jesus, I hope in you"?

CAN YOU ALSO ANSWER THIS?

319 What will confirmation do for you?

REVIEW QUESTIONS

Why did God make you?

What must you do to be happy with God in heaven?

How does Jesus help all men to gain heaven?

How does the Catholic Church help us to gain heaven?

What is a sacrament?

O Jesus, I love you with all my heart

We sometimes wish that Jesus had not gone back to heaven. We think of those little children who could climb right on his lap. But we forget that he is still on earth.

Jesus becomes present in the Holy Eucharist in every Mass. Jesus is truly with us in the Blessed

Sacrament. The Blessed Sacrament is in the tabernacle in the church.

And why does Jesus live there? Just because he loves us so much, and wants to be where he can help us more and more.

Jesus likes to have us visit him. When we come, he blesses us as he did those little children many years ago.

But Jesus likes most of all to have us receive him in Holy Communion. In Holy Communion Jesus comes right into our heart. We can talk to him as to our dearest friend.

"O Jesus, I love you with all my heart."

I receive Jesus in the sacrament of the Holy Eucharist when I receive Holy Communion. I do not see Jesus Christ in the Holy Eucharist because he is hidden under the appearances of bread and wine.

To receive Holy Communion I must:

1 Have my soul free from mortal sin.
2 Not eat or drink anything for one hour before receiving Holy Communion. But water may be taken at any time before Holy Communion.

Before Holy Communion I should:
1 Think of Jesus.
2 Sing and pray with all the other people at Mass.
3 Say the prayers I have learned.
4 Ask Jesus to come to me.

After Holy Communion I should:
1 Thank Jesus for coming to me.
2 Tell him how much I love him.
3 Ask him to help me.
4 Pray for others.

One of the best ways to grow closer to Jesus is to receive him in Holy Communion as often as we can. Jesus will help us to be better persons and he will unite us more closely with all the members of the Church, God's family on earth.

HOW MANY CAN YOU ANSWER?

320 Why do we sometimes wish that Jesus had not gone back to heaven?
321 When does Jesus become present in the Holy Eucharist?
322 What is the tabernacle?
323 Why does Jesus stay with us in the Blessed Sacrament?

324 Why should we visit Jesus present in the Blessed Sacrament?

325 What does Jesus do for us when we visit him in church?

326 How can we please Jesus even more than by visiting him?

327 When Jesus comes to us in Holy Communion, how does he like to have us talk to him?

328 What little prayer can you say to tell Jesus that you love him?

CAN YOU ALSO ANSWER THESE?

329 Do you receive Jesus Christ in the sacrament of the Holy Eucharist?

330 Do you see Jesus Christ in the Holy Eucharist?

331 What must you do to receive Holy Communion?

332 What should you do before Holy Communion?

333 What should you do after Holy Communion?

REVIEW QUESTIONS

What is the sacrament of the Holy Eucharist?
When does Jesus Christ become present in the Holy Eucharist?

NOTE. You can learn much more about questions 329 to 333 if you study pages 117 to 123 and 128 to 131.

On the next page begins the nicest part of this book. It is all about a little child who tells us what he thinks and what he does when he goes to confession and Holy Communion.

The little child is called I. Who do you think he (or she) is?

Come, O Holy Spirit, help me

We can show Jesus how much we love him and all that we have learned so far by the way we go to confession and Holy Communion. Jesus sees each one of us. He sees me. And this is what he likes to see me do.

97

MEETING JESUS IN THE
SACRAMENT OF FORGIVENESS

I remember how Jesus said to his apostles that first Easter Day, "Receive the Holy Spirit. Whose sins you shall forgive they are forgiven them." It was then that Jesus gave us the great gift of the sacrament of penance to make us happy and at peace. When we receive the sacrament of penance Jesus not only takes away our sins but helps us to be good.

When I want to go to confession, I go to the church. I kneel down and pray. Sometimes I pray from a prayer book, but often I pray just from my heart. I tell Jesus that I am sorry for having sinned. I ask him to help me to make a good confession. I ask Mary and my Guardian Angel to help me too. Then I say this little prayer:

Come, O Holy Spirit, help me:
to think of my sins,
to be heartily sorry for them,
to make up my mind to do them no more,
to tell them to the priest, and
to do my penance.

This little prayer to the Holy Spirit helps me to remember the five things I should do to make a good confession.

HOW MANY CAN YOU ANSWER?

334 What gift did Jesus give us on the first Easter Day?

335 What does Jesus do for us in confession?

336 What do you do when you go to confession?

337 How do you pray?

338 What do you ask Jesus?

339 Whom else can you ask for help?

340 Why should we pray to the Holy Spirit?

341 What will the prayer to the Holy Spirit help us to remember?

To think of my sins

1 To think of my sins

I think of my sins by trying to remember what I did that was wrong since my last confession. I know something was wrong if by what I did I hurt others and did not show that I loved them. To help me remember what I ought to remember, I learned a little rhyme. This is the rhyme:

Think of God, his name, and day;
Parents, too, who care for you.
Are you kind in every way?
Pure, and honest, truthful, too?

The words in this rhyme help me to remember the sins that are on the list on pages 124-26 of this book.

When I recall a sin that I have committed, I see if I can tell it in just a few words. If I want to, I can say about how many times I did it. Most of our sins we can tell very quickly; like this, "I told a lie about three times."

We can also tell our sins in another way. We can say what we did that was wrong and then tell why we did it. We can say it like this, "I told a lie because I was ashamed of what I did"; or, "I told a lie because I was afraid of being punished." "I disobeyed my parents because I was lazy"; or, "I disobeyed my parents because I was stubborn." "I fought with others because I wanted my way"; or, "I fought with others because I lost my temper."

I do not worry if I cannot remember everything. I know that the only sins we have to tell are sins that we can remember and are really big. Jesus knows how easy it is to forget. Jesus also knows that most little boys and girls have not done anything that is really a big sin.

HOW MANY CAN YOU ANSWER?

342 What is the first thing you should do to make a good confession?

343 How do you think of your sins?

344 What have you learned to help you remember what you ought to remember?

345 What is this little rhyme?

346 What do you do when you recall a sin that you committed?

347 How can you tell most of your sins?

348 Besides confessing what we did that was wrong, what else can we tell the priest about our sins?

349 Why do you not worry if you cannot remember everything?

350 What two things does Jesus know about us that should keep us from worrying?

To be heartily sorry for them

If I found a big sin on my soul, it would make me very sorry to think that I offended Jesus so much. But it would not make me afraid to tell it. Jesus gave us the sacrament of penance just so we could tell our sins and have them forgiven.

How much Jesus suffered the night he prayed in the garden and saw the sins of the whole world!

How much he wants to have all those sins told in confession!

The priest is glad when we tell him our sins because he wants to take them away. To hide a serious sin from the priest just puts another big sin on our soul. And the next time we go to confession we have to tell what we did and make our confession all over again. The priest will die before he lets anyone know a single sin we tell him.

If I cannot think of any real sin since my last confession, I can say to the priest, "Father, I cannot think of any real sin since my last confession. This is a sin from my past life ...." And then I tell him an old sin for which I am very sorry.

I receive special grace to live a good Christian life every time I meet Jesus in the sacrament of penance. I may want to go to confession every week, every two weeks, or once a month. I may go to confession as often as the priest thinks best.

351 What would you do if you found that you had committed a big sin?

352 Why would you be sorry for the sin?

353 Why would you not be afraid to tell it in confession?

354 Why is the priest glad when we tell him our sins?

355 What kind of a sin does a person commit if he hides a big sin from the priest?

356 If we have hidden a serious sin from the priest, what must we do the next time we go to confession?

357 What would a priest do before he would let anyone know the sins we tell him?

358 What may you do if you want to meet Jesus in the sacrament of forgiveness but cannot think of any real sin since your last confession?

359 What kind of help does Jesus give you every time you receive the sacrament of penance?

360 How often may you go to confession?

To make up my mind to do them no more

Sometimes things happen that are not sins at all.
It is not a sin to miss Mass on Sunday when we cannot help it. It is not a sin to have bad thoughts when
we do not want to have those thoughts. It is not a
sin for me if I do something when I do not know it
is a sin. I do not have to tell such things in confession. But if anything ever worried me, I would ask

the priest about it. And afterwards I would do just as the priest told me.

If I do not know how to tell a sin, I can say, "Father, I have a sin I do not know how to tell." And then the priest will help me.

2 To be heartily sorry for them

3 To make up my mind to do them no more

The night before Jesus died, his enemies put him on trial. Peter, one of the apostles, waited outside for the trial to be over. While he was waiting some of the people said he was a friend of Jesus. Peter kept telling them that he did not even know Jesus.

A cock crowed and reminded Peter of something Jesus had told him at the Last Supper. He thought of how he had sinned against Jesus. Peter was so sorry that he wept bitterly. After I think of how I sinned against Jesus, I want to be sorry too.

HOW MANY CAN YOU ANSWER?

361 What are some of the things that can happen that are not sins?

362 Why do I not have to tell these things
in confession?

363 What could you do if you were worried about
something you had done?

364 What can you do if you do not know how to
tell a sin?

365 What is the second thing you should do to make a
good confession?

366 What is the third thing?

367 After Peter thought of how he had sinned against
Jesus, how did he feel?

368 How should we feel when we think of our sins?

To tell them to the priest

I make an act of contrition. It is the prayer that begins: "O my God, I am heartily sorry." I say that prayer very slowly. I mean every word of it.

I think of how one big sin can make a person lose heaven and go to hell; and how one little sin can make me go to purgatory. I think of how every sin offends Jesus, who is so good, and made him die on

109

the cross. And then I make up my mind to sin no more. Jesus cannot forgive our sins if we are not sorry for them, or if we want to do them again.

4 To tell them to the priest

While I wait my turn to go to confession, I think of what I am going to do. I am going to see the priest who takes the place of Jesus. He will take away my sins, and the sacrament will give me strength to be good.

When it is my turn, I walk in and kneel down. I begin when the priest opens the little door. I stand up if I am too little to talk through the little door. I talk just loud enough for the priest alone to hear.

HOW MANY CAN YOU ANSWER?

369 What is the act of contrition?
370 How do you say that prayer?
371 How much of that prayer do you mean?
372 What kind of punishment could you receive for sinning?
373 What made Jesus die on the cross?
374 When will Jesus forgive our sins?

375 What is the fourth thing you should do to make a good confession?
376 What do you do while you wait for your turn to go to confession?
377 Whom are you going to see?
378 What will he do?
379 What do you do when it is your turn?
380 When do you begin to tell your sins?
381 What should you do if you are too little to talk through the little door?
382 How loudly do you talk?

And to do my penance

Jesus loved to tell this story about the shepherd and the lost sheep. He said there was a man who had one hundred sheep. One of those little sheep strayed away from the rest and was in danger. The good shepherd left all the other ninety-nine sheep in the pasture and went to find the missing sheep. And when he had found the missing sheep, the good shepherd joyfully took it right up on his shoulders. He told his friends and the other shepherds how happy he was because he had found the lost sheep.

Jesus is a good shepherd and we are his sheep. He loves to keep us safe with him. But if we stray away because of sin, Jesus does not rest until we come back to him. In the sacrament of forgiveness, Jesus leads me back to being a good child of God and a strong Christian.

When the priest opens the little door, I make the sign of the cross and say, "Bless me, Father. I have sinned. My last confession was ...." (Here I tell him when.) And right away I tell him my sins. After the last sin, I say, "I am sorry for these sins and the sins of my whole life, especially for ...." (And here I name a past sin for which I am very sorry.)

Then I listen to what the priest says. I listen to him just as I would to Jesus. He tells me what I should do for my penance. And then he may tell me to make an act of contrition. That means I say again with all my heart the prayer that begins: "O my God, I am heartily sorry." If the priest does not tell me to say the act of contrition, I listen to him as he prays and says the words that take away my sins. In my heart I tell God I am sorry. When it is time to leave, the priest may say, "God bless you" or "Go in peace." And I answer, "Thank you, Father."

5 And to do my penance

If my penance is to say a prayer, I pray it right away so that I will not forget it. If my penance is to do something, like being kind to the brother I had a fight with, I will remember to do it as soon as there is a chance.

Besides saying my penance, I take some time to talk to Jesus and to thank him for forgiving me. I can tell him that I feel as close to him and as happy and peaceful as a lost sheep when it is safely in the arms of the shepherd who found it.

I thank the Holy Spirit. I thank Mary and my Guardian Angel. I also ask them to keep me good from now on.

I do not worry if I find that I forgot to tell something. When we try to make a good confession, Jesus forgives all our sins whether we remembered them all or not. Even if we forgot a very big sin, we can go to Holy Communion. All we have to do is tell that big sin in our next confession.

After we have told a sin in a good confession, we never have to tell it again.

Jesus and Mary and all the angels and saints love me very much. Jesus wants to come into my heart. He wants to strengthen me with his life so that I will be a good Christian. Jesus wants me to be a happy, strong member of God's family. After a good confession I am strong again.

HOW MANY CAN YOU ANSWER?

383 Why did the good shepherd leave the ninety-nine sheep alone in the pasture?
384 What did he do when he found the missing sheep?
385 Who is the shepherd and who are the sheep?
386 When are we like the sheep that was lost?
387 When are we like the sheep after it had been found?
388 What do you do in the confessional when the priest opens the little door?
389 What do you say after you have confessed your sins?
390 What is one thing the priest always tells you to do?

391 What prayer do you say if Father tells you to make an act of contrition?

392 What should you do if Father does not tell you to make an act of contrition?

393 What does the priest say when it is time to leave?

394 And what do you answer?

395 What is the fifth thing you should do to make a good confession?

396 When do you say your penance?

397 Besides saying your penance what should you take some time to do after confession?

398 To whom can you talk besides Jesus?

399 What does Jesus do when we try to make a good confession?

400 If we forgot a big sin, could we go to Holy Communion?

401 But what would we have to do about that big sin?

402 After we have told a sin in a good confession, do we ever have to tell it again?

O Sacrament most holy! O Sacrament divine!

MEETING JESUS IN THE SACRAMENT OF HIS LOVE

Jesus wanted to give me himself in Holy Communion. Just as food keeps my body strong, Jesus gives me himself in Holy Communion to keep my soul strong.

117

I fast before Holy Communion

I must not eat or drink anything for one hour before receiving Holy Communion. Water may be taken any time before Holy Communion. And the sick may always take medicine.

I get to Mass on time

In the morning I think of Jesus. I hurry off to church. I always want to get to Mass on time. I remember that Holy Communion is the sacrament of Jesus' love. I know it is just like being at the Last Supper when Jesus first gave the Blessed Sacrament to the apostles.

I know that Jesus is coming

The priest will take bread and wine. He will say, "This is my body. . . . This is my blood," and right away the bread and wine will become the body and blood of Jesus.

I pray

In a little while I know that the priest will give me the body and blood of Jesus in Holy Communion. So I keep praying. Sometimes I pray by singing with all the people at Mass. Sometimes I say the prayers in my prayer book. Sometimes I say little prayers just from my heart.

HOW MANY CAN YOU ANSWER?

403 Why does Jesus want to give himself to you in Holy Communion?

404 How long must you fast before Holy Communion?

405 What may you drink any time before Holy Communion?

406 Why may you receive Holy Communion if you take medicine before you go to church?

407 Whom and what should you think about on your way to Mass?

408 How soon do you want to get to church?

409 What is being at Mass like?

410 What will the priest do at Mass?

411 What will happen as soon as he says, "This is my body. . . . This is my blood"?

412 How do you pray before Holy Communion?

All praise and all thanksgiving be every moment thine

As the time to receive Jesus comes closer, I say to him, "O Jesus, I believe in you. O Jesus, I hope in you. O Jesus, I love you with all my heart. Come to me, dear Jesus, I want so much to receive you."

I go to receive Jesus

When the happy time comes, I go to receive Holy Communion. I do not want to think of anything but Jesus. When the priest, or someone who takes his place, comes to me, I lift my head and look at the host. Father says, "Body of Christ," and I say, "Amen." I receive the host and eat it. The host looks and tastes like bread, but it is not bread. It is Jesus! It is the same Jesus who was born in the stable, who blessed the little children, and who gave the apostles Holy Communion at the Last Supper.

At special times, the cup used at Mass is offered to me. I take a sip from the chalice. It looks and tastes like wine, but it is not wine. It is Jesus.

HOW MANY CAN YOU ANSWER?

413 What do you say to Jesus?
414 Where do you go when the happy time comes?
415 What do you think of?
416 What do you do when the priest comes to you?
417 What does Father, or the one who takes his place, say as he holds the host?
418 What do you answer?
419 How does the host look and taste?
420 But what is it?
421 What do you do with the host after you receive it?
422 At special times what may I receive?

I thank Jesus

I go back to my place and kneel down again. I am glad that Jesus is with me. He is my best friend. I talk to him. I thank him for having come to me.

I ask him to help me

I ask him to help me and bless me. I beg him to keep me good. I say again and again, "O Jesus, I believe in you. O Jesus, I hope in you. O Jesus, I love you with all my heart. I thank you for having come to me. O dear Jesus, keep me good."

I pray for everyone

I tell him to help my mother and father, my brothers and sisters, our priests and teachers. I also pray for all people who belong to God's family and those who do not. I say the Prayer to Jesus Crucified for the suffering souls in purgatory.

And

Before I go home I say a little prayer to the Mother of Jesus. I tell Mary that Jesus has come to me. I ask her to keep me good until he comes again.

423 Why are you happy after receiving
Holy Communion?

424 What do you tell Jesus after he comes to you?

425 What do you ask Jesus to do for you?

426 What prayer can you say again and again?

427 Whom else do you ask Jesus to help?

428 Do you know the Prayer to Jesus Crucified? If not,
find it on pages 130 and 131.

429 For whom do you say the
Prayer to Jesus Crucified?

430 What do you do before you go home?

431 What do you tell her?

432 What do you ask her?

WHEN I GO TO CONFESSION

Dear Jesus, I have sinned. But now I am sorry. I want to go to confession. I know that if I make a good confession, you will take away my sins and help me to be good. Jesus, please help me to make a good confession. Mary, my dear mother, help me to make my soul pure and beautiful like yours. My Guardian Angel, pray for me.

Prayer to the Holy Spirit

Come, O Holy Spirit, help me:
to think of my sins,
to be heartily sorry for them,
to make up my mind to do them no more,
to tell them to the priest, and
to do my penance.

1 To think of my sins

(When I remember a sin that I committed, I see if I can tell it in just a few words. I may also tell how many times I committed a sin and the reason why.)

1 GOD   Did I refuse to say my prayers when I knew I should say them? Or did I hurry through them? How often?

2 NAME   Did I use holy names like Jesus and God when I should not have used them?

3 DAY   Did I miss Mass on Sunday through my own fault? Or did I come late? How late? Did I misbehave in church?

4 PARENTS   Did I sin by not obeying my parents, teachers, or others who had charge of me? Was I mean to them? Was I lazy? Was I stubborn? Did I answer back? Did I make fun of old people?

5 BE KIND   Did I hate anyone? Did I do anything mean to anyone? Did I let myself get angry and call anyone mean names? Did I quarrel and fight? Did I wish anything mean to anyone? Did I make anyone sin?

6 BE PURE   (Sometimes little children call things impure that are not impure at all. I should not say I did anything impure unless I am sure of it.) Did I do anything that was really impure? Was it alone or with others? Did I willingly keep impure thoughts in my mind? Did I sin by using impure

words? Did I sin by looking at or reading anything impure? Did I sin by talking about or listening to anything impure?

7 BE HONEST   Did I steal anything? What was it? Did I keep anything that did not belong to me? Did I break or hurt anything because I was mean or did not care? What was it?

8 BE TRUTHFUL   Did I tell any lies? Did I tell mean things about anyone? Did I sin by listening to people say mean things about anyone? Did I willingly keep mean thoughts in my mind?

Is there anything else I did that was a sin? In church? In school? At home? At play? Is there anything that worries me? Is there anything I should ask the priest about?

2 To be heartily sorry for them

3 To make up my mind to do them no more

Dear Jesus, I seem to see you hanging on the cross. I know my sins have put you there. I am really sorry and do not want to sin again. Please listen to me as I slowly say my act of contrition.

"O my God, I am heartily sorry for having offended thee, and I detest all my sins, because of thy just punishments, but most of all because they offend thee, my God, who art all-good and deserving of all my love. I firmly resolve, with the help of thy grace, to sin no more and to avoid the near occasions of sin."

4 To tell them to the priest

Bless me, Father. I have sinned. My last confession was ....

I .... about .... times.

I am sorry for these sins and the sins of my whole life, especially for ....

Thank you, Father.

5 And to do my penance

Dear Jesus, I want to do something to make up for my sins. Please help me to do my penance well. I am going to do it right away.

I thank you, Jesus, for having taken away my sins. Dear Holy Spirit, dear Mother of God, dear Guardian Angel, I thank you all for helping me to make a good confession. I want to be good from now on.

WHEN I GO
TO HOLY COMMUNION

Before Holy Communion

O Jesus, I believe in you. O Jesus, I hope in you. O Jesus, I love you with all my heart. Come to me, dear Jesus, I want so much to receive you.

And now, dear Jesus, let me talk to you in my own words.

I remember how happy the shepherds were. They saw you as a tiny baby in the stable at Bethlehem.

I remember how happy Mary and Joseph were. They saw you as a little child in their home at Nazareth.

I remember how happy those children were. They saw you and climbed right on your lap.

But how much happier should I be, dear Jesus! You are coming right into my heart!

Holy Mary, you never had a sin on your soul. How I wish I had a soul like yours! How much nicer it would be when Jesus comes to me.

Dear Jesus, I am sorry for all my sins. I am not good enough for you to come to me.

My good Guardian Angel, help me to be as good as I can be. Holy Mary, pray for me. Be with me when Jesus comes.

O Jesus, I believe in you. O Jesus, I hope in you. O Jesus, I love you with all my heart. Come to me, dear Jesus, I want so much to receive you.

After Holy Communion

O Jesus, I believe in you. O Jesus, I hope in you. O Jesus, I love you with all my heart. I thank you for having come to me. Welcome, my best friend!

You are the same Jesus who was born in the stable at Bethlehem. You are the same Jesus who loved Mary and Joseph and helped them all you could. You are the same Jesus who loved little children and let them come to you. You are the same Jesus who gave Holy Communion to the apostles at the Last Supper. You are the same Jesus who died for us all on the cross. And now you have come to me! Oh, how can I thank you!

O Sacrament most holy! O Sacrament divine! All praise and all thanksgiving be every moment thine.

Dear Jesus, you even said that I could ask you for anything I want. I now ask you to help my mother and father, my brothers and sisters, our priests and teachers, and everyone. Help also the suffering souls in purgatory, and take them to heaven.

Holy Mary, you are the Mother of Jesus. You so often held him in your arms. He is now in my heart. You know what to do and what to say. Come, be with me while he is here. Adore him, love him, and thank him for me.

Dear Mother, Jesus wants me to be good. Please help me. Help me to say my prayers every day. Help me to do what I am told. Help me to be always kind, honest, and truthful. Keep me from all sin. Keep me good until Jesus comes again.

PRAYER TO JESUS CRUCIFIED

Look down upon me, good and gentle Jesus, while before thy face I humbly kneel, and with burning soul pray and beseech thee to fix deep in my heart lively sentiments of faith, hope, and charity, true contrition for my sins and a firm purpose of amendment; and while I contemplate with great love and tender pity thy five wounds, pondering over them within me, and calling to mind the words which David, thy prophet, said of thee, my Jesus, "They have pierced my hands and my feet; they have numbered all my bones."

(One Our Father, Hail Mary, and Glory Be to the Father, for our Holy Father, the pope.)

FIRST COMMUNION QUESTIONS—
A REVIEW

1 Who made you?
God made me.

2 Did God make all things?
Yes, God made all things.

3 Why did God make you?
God made me to show his goodness and to make me
happy with him in heaven.

4 What must you do to be happy with God in heaven?
To be happy with God in heaven I must know him,
love him, and serve him in this world.

5 Where is God?
God is everywhere.

6 Does God know all things?
Yes, God knows all things.

7 Can God do all things?
Yes, God can do all things.

8 Did God have a beginning?
No, God had no beginning; he always was.

9 Will God always be?
Yes, God will always be.

10 Is there only one God?
Yes, there is only one God.

11 How many Persons are there in God?
In God there are three Persons—the Father, the Son, and the Holy Spirit.

12 What do we call the three Persons in one God?
We call the three Persons in one God the Blessed Trinity.

13 How do we know that there are three Persons in one God?
We know that there are three Persons in one God because we have God's word for it.

14 Did one of the Persons of the Blessed Trinity become man?
Yes, the Second Person, the Son of God, became man.

15 What is the name of the Son of God made man?
The name of the Son of God made man is Jesus Christ.

16 When was Jesus born?
Jesus was born on the first Christmas Day, more than nineteen hundred years ago.

17 Who is the Mother of Jesus?
The Mother of Jesus is the Blessed Virgin Mary.

18 Is Jesus Christ both God and man?
Yes, Jesus Christ is both God and man.

19 Why did God the Son become man?
God the Son became man to satisfy for the sins of all men and to help everybody to gain heaven.

20 How did Jesus satisfy for the sins of all men?
Jesus satisfied for the sins of all men by his sufferings and death on the cross.

21 How does Jesus help all men to gain heaven?
Jesus helps all men to gain heaven through the Catholic Church.

22 What is sin?
Sin is disobedience to God's laws.

23 Who committed the first sin?
The bad angels committed the first sin.

24 Who committed the first sin on earth?
Our first parents, Adam and Eve, committed the first sin on earth.

25 Is this sin passed on to us from Adam?
Yes, this sin is passed on to us from Adam.

26 What is this sin in us called?
This sin in us is called original sin.

27 Was anyone ever free from original sin?
The Blessed Virgin Mary was free from original sin.

28 Is original sin the only kind of sin?
No, there is another kind of sin, called actual sin.

29 What is actual sin?
Actual sin is any sin which we ourselves commit.

30 How many kinds of actual sin are there?
There are two kinds of actual sin: mortal sin and venial sin.

31 What is mortal sin?
Mortal sin is a deadly sin.

32 What does mortal sin do to us?
Mortal sin makes us enemies of God and robs us of his life, sanctifying grace.

33 What happens to those who die in mortal sin?
Those who die in mortal sin are punished forever in hell.

34 What is venial sin?
Venial sin is a lesser sin.

35 Does venial sin make us enemies of God or rob our souls of his life?
No, venial sin does not make us enemies of God or rob our souls of his life.

36 Does venial sin displease God?
Yes, venial sin does displease God.

37 How does the Catholic Church help us to gain heaven?
The Catholic Church helps us to gain heaven especially through the sacraments.

38 What is a sacrament?
A sacrament is an outward sign, instituted by Christ to give grace.

39 What does grace do to the soul?
Grace makes the soul holy and pleasing to God.

40 What sacrament have you received?
I have received the sacrament of baptism.

41 What did baptism do for you?
Baptism washed away original sin from my soul and made it rich in the grace of God.

42 Are you preparing to receive other sacraments?
I am preparing to receive the sacraments of penance, Holy Eucharist, and confirmation.

43 What will confirmation do for you?
Confirmation, through the coming of the Holy Spirit, will make me a witness of Jesus Christ.

44 What is the sacrament of penance?
The sacrament of penance is the sacrament by which sins committed after baptism are forgiven.

45 What must you do to receive the sacrament of penance?
To receive the sacrament of penance I must:
1 Find out my sins.
2 Be sorry for my sins.
3 Make up my mind not to sin again.
4 Tell my sins to the priest.
5 Do the penance the priest gives me.

46 How do you make your confession?
I make my confession in this way:
1 I go into the confessional and kneel.

2 I make the sign of the cross and say, "Bless me, Father. I have sinned."

3 I say, "This is my first confession" (or, "It has been a week, or a month, or ...., since my last confession").

4 I confess my sins.

5 I listen to what the priest tells me.

6 I say the act of contrition or listen to the words of absolution. This depends on the priest and on what he wants me to do.

47 What do you do after leaving the confessional?
After leaving the confessional, I thank God for forgiving my sins. I say the prayers which the priest gave me as a penance. If my penance is to do some act, I ask God to help me remember to do it as soon as I have a chance.

48 What is the sacrament of the Holy Eucharist?
The Holy Eucharist is the sacrament of the body and blood of our Lord Jesus Christ.

49 When does Jesus Christ become present in the Holy Eucharist?
Jesus Christ becomes present in the Holy Eucharist during the sacrifice of the Mass.

50 Do you receive Jesus Christ in the sacrament of the Holy Eucharist?
I receive Jesus Christ in the sacrament of the Holy Eucharist when I receive Holy Communion.

51 Do you see Jesus Christ in the Holy Eucharist?
No, I do not see Jesus Christ in the Holy Eucharist
because he is hidden under the appearances of
bread and wine.

52 What must you do to receive Holy Communion?
To receive Holy Communion I must:
1 Have my soul free from mortal sin.
2 Not eat or drink anything for one hour before
receiving Holy Communion. But water may be
taken at any time before Holy Communion.

53 What should you do before Holy Communion?
Before Holy Communion I should:
1 Think of Jesus.
2 Sing and pray with all the other people at Mass.
3 Say the prayers I have learned.
4 Ask Jesus to come to me.

54 What should you do after Holy Communion?
After Holy Communion I should:
1 Thank Jesus for coming to me.
2 Tell him how much I love him.
3 Ask him to help me.
4 Pray for others.